REAL WORLD DATA

GRAPHING WATER

Sarah Medina

Heinemann
LIBRARY

www.heinemann.co.uk/library
Visit our website to find out more information about **Heinemann Library** books.

To order:
 Phone 44 (0) 1865 888066
 Send a fax to 44 (0) 1865 314091
Visit the Heinemann Bookshop at www.heinemann.co.uk/library to browse our catalogue and order online.

Heinemann Library is an imprint of Pearson Education Limited, a company incorporated in England and Wales having its registered office at Edinburgh Gate, Harlow, Essex, CM20 2JE – Registered company number: 00872828
Heinemann Library is a registered trademark of Pearson Education Limited
Text © Pearson Education Ltd 2009
First published in paperback in 2009
The moral rights of the proprietor have been asserted.

Edited by Nancy Dickmann and Rachel Howells
Designed by Victoria Bevan and Geoff Ward
Original illustrations© Pearson Education Ltd
Illustrations by Geoff Ward
Picture research by Hannah Taylor
Originated by Modern Age
Printed and bound in China by Leo Paper Group

ISBN 978 0 431 02944 3 (hardback)
13 12 11 10 09
10 9 8 7 6 5 4 3 2 1

ISBN 978 0 431 02958 0 (paperback)
13 12 11 10 09
10 9 8 7 6 5 4 3 2 1

British Library Cataloguing in Publication Data
Medina, Sarah,
Graphing water. - (Real world data)
551.4'6'0728

A full catalogue record for this book is available from the British Library.

Acknowledgements
The publishers would like to thank the following for permission to reproduce photographs: ©Alamy p.**16** (Suzanne Porter); ©Corbis pp. **8 bottom** (Blaine Harrington III), **11 top** (Paul Souders), **12** (Nevada Wier), **14 right** (Imageshop), **14 left** (Randy Faris), **25** (Anna Clopet); ©Getty Images pp. **8 top** (AFP/ Narinder Nanu), **11 bottom** (Photographer's Choice/Cameron Davidson), **22** (Photographer's Choice/Grant Faint); ©naturepl.com pp. **6** (David Noton), **20** (David Tipling); ©Science Photo Library pp. **5** (Veronique Leplat), **18** (George Steinmetz), **24** (Simon Fraser); ©Still Pictures pp. **26** (Sean Sprague), **27** (Mark Edwards).

Cover photograph of Akita Prefecture, Japan, reproduced with permission of ©Getty Images/ Sebun Photo (Nobuaki Sumida).

The publishers would like to thank Harold Pratt for his assistance in the preparation of this book.

Every effort has been made to contact copyright holders of any material reproduced in this book. Any omissions will be rectified in subsequent printings if notice is given to the publishers.

Disclaimer
All the internet addresses (URLs) given in this book were valid at time of going to press.

CONTENTS

Some words are printed in bold, **like this**. You can find out what they mean by looking in the glossary, on page 30.

WHAT IS WATER?

Water is a **liquid**, which has no colour, taste, or smell. It may seem commonplace, but it is really special – and very important. Up to 70 percent of the human body is made up of water!

Water is found all over the Earth. More than 70 percent of the Earth's surface is covered in water. The water on Earth is continually changing its form. Water is found as liquid in rivers, lakes, and oceans. It is found as a **gas** in **water vapour**. Water is also found in **solid** form, for example, as ice and **glaciers** on mountains.

What are graphs?
This book uses graphs to show information about water. Graphs are a way to show information visually. There are many different types of graphs, but all graphs make it easier to see patterns at a glance.

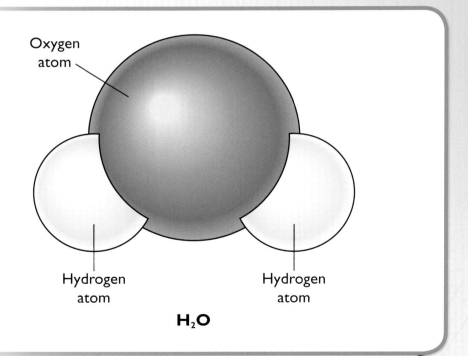

Oxygen atom

Hydrogen atom

Hydrogen atom

H_2O

 Water is also known as H_2O. This is because each water **molecule** is made up of two **hydrogen atoms** (H_2) and one **oxygen** atom (O).

 We all need to drink plenty of water for our bodies to stay healthy.

Water equals life

Without water, nothing could survive on Earth. Plants and animals – and humans – would all die if there were no water.

Everyone needs water to survive and be healthy. Humans get most of their water from drinks, such as plain water or other drinks which include water. They also get water from eating food. Some food, especially fruit and vegetables, contains a lot of water – even though it is not obvious. We also use water for many other things, including washing, cooking, and growing food.

Without water, life would be impossible. Although humans can survive for up to three weeks without food, they would die after only three days without a drink!

THE EARTH'S WATER

Water moves around, through, and above the Earth constantly, in the form of **water vapour**, liquid, and ice. The same water is continually recycled, in what is called the **water cycle**. This means that the same water that is on the Earth today was here millions of years ago!

Nearly three-quarters of the Earth is covered with water. Most of this is in the oceans. Ocean water is salt water, which means that the water is mixed with salt. We cannot use this water for drinking or growing crops.

 Most of the Earth is covered with salt water in the oceans.

The rest of the Earth's water is fresh water, which contains very little salt. Most fresh water is ice, which is found mainly in **glaciers** and **icecaps** in the Earth's **polar regions**. **Groundwater** is fresh water that is trapped in the ground, sometimes deep below the surface. Some fresh water is found in rocks, known as **aquifers**. Most of the fresh water we see is in rivers, lakes, and **swamps**. Fresh water for human use is often stored in artificial lakes, called reservoirs.

Land and water

The table below shows the percentage of the Earth's surface that is covered by land and by water. A type of graph called a pie chart can show the same information visually. A pie chart shows the different parts of a whole picture. The blue section of the pie chart shows that 71 percent of the Earth's surface is covered with water. The green section shows that the rest (29 percent) is covered with land. We can now see quickly that there is much more water than land!

Surface structure	Percentage (%) of Earth's surface
Water	71
Land	29
Total	100

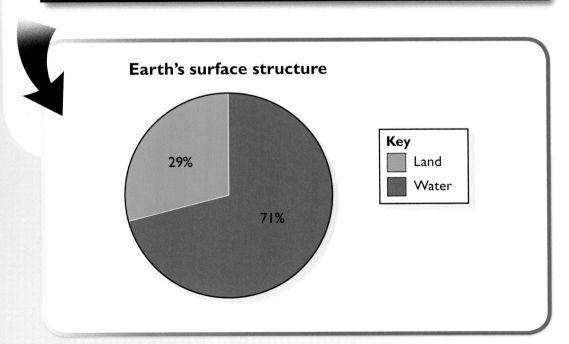

Earth's surface structure

Key
Land
Water

Every living thing needs water to survive. However, some parts of the world have more water than others. In countries where there is little water, plants, animals, and people can find life a struggle.

Precipitation is water that falls from the air to the ground. Rain, sleet, hailstones, and snow are all types of precipitation. Across the world, 5,000 billion tonnes of precipitation falls to the ground every year! Precipitation is important, because it helps to fill up rivers and lakes with fresh water, and it is part of the **water cycle**.

Different parts of the world have different levels of precipitation. Some places receive a lot of rain, and others receive barely any. The driest places on Earth are called deserts.

 In India lots of water falls as rain during the monsoon season.

Drought and floods

The amount of precipitation is not always the same. When there is far less rain than usual, this is called a **drought**. In a drought, it is hard for people to grow food, because plants cannot grow without water. **Floods** happen when too much rain falls at one time. Rivers can spill over and cover the land. Floods can be very dangerous, killing plants, animals, and people.

 The Atacama desert in Chile is one of the driest places on Earth.

Bar charts

The table below lists the average amount of rain in some of the world's cities. The bar chart shows this information in visual form. A bar chart is a type of graph that is useful to compare information, such as amounts. On the bar chart, the horizontal line (called the **x-axis**) shows the names of the cities. The vertical line (called the **y-axis**) shows how many millimetres of rain fell in one year. You can see at a glance that the city with the tallest bar (Tokyo) had the most rain.

City	Average rainfall per year (mm)
Tokyo, Japan	1523
Sydney, Australia	1223
New York, USA	1129
Toronto, Canada	817
London, UK	611
Miami, USA	490
Madrid, Spain	439
Athens, Greece	371

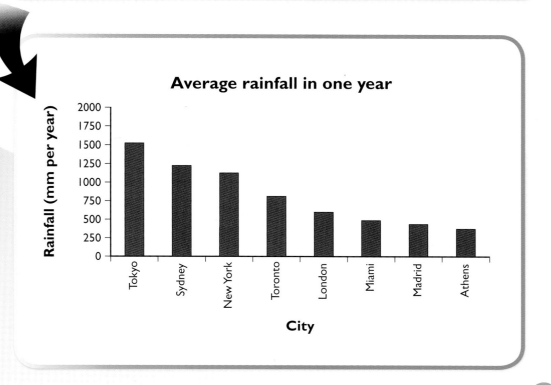

THE WATER CYCLE

The Earth's water is constantly being recycled. This happens because of a process called the **water cycle**. In the water cycle, water travels from the surface of the Earth to the air, and then back to the Earth again. During this process, water changes its form.

First, the sun heats up the water in oceans, lakes, and rivers. Some of the water **evaporates**, rising into the air as **water vapour**. Trees, other plants, and soil also release a very small amount of water, also as water vapour. This is known as **transpiration**.

The water vapour that rises up from the Earth cools down in the air. When it gets cool enough it **condenses**, forming clouds. The clouds then produce **precipitation**, which falls back to the ground. About three-quarters of the precipitation falls into the oceans. The rest falls onto land.

Some of the water that falls on land soaks into the ground, topping up **groundwater** levels. Plants use some of this water to grow. Most of the water, however, eventually flows downhill into lakes and rivers, and back into the ocean. This process is called **run-off**. Then the water evaporates and the cycle starts again.

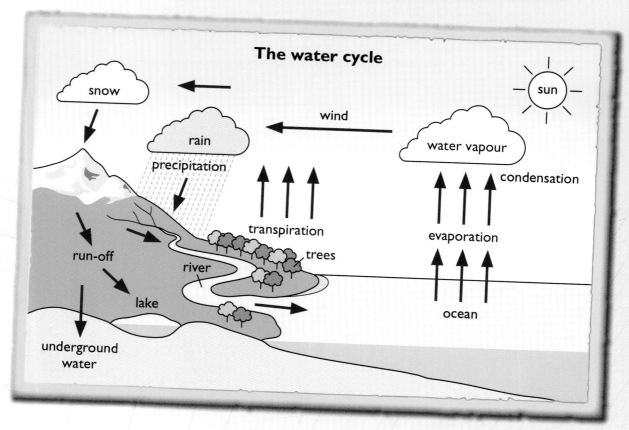

The water cycle

snow

wind

rain

precipitation

transpiration

trees

sun

water vapour

condensation

evaporation

run-off

river

lake

ocean

underground water

Water in icecaps can take thousands of years to go back into oceans as part of the water cycle.

Salty water!

During run-off, water flows back into the world's oceans. As water flows in rivers, it collects tiny amounts of salt from rocks and soil in the river. When water evaporates from the ocean during the water cycle, the salt is left behind, because salt does not evaporate. The water that is left in the ocean gets saltier until it is diluted again by precipitation or melting ice.

Some water from precipitation gradually makes its way into rivers and then into oceans.

WATER FOR LIFE

All living things depend on water. Where water is scarce, life is hard. Yet only 3 percent of all the water on Earth is suitable for human use.

One of the main uses of water is for farming. Water is needed to grow crops such as rice, and for animals to drink. Water is also used in **industry**, to make products, such as paper, and to supply electricity to run lights and many products. Home use is the third most important use of water. People at home use water for drinking, cooking, washing, and cleaning.

Around the world, our water needs are different. Different percentages of water are used for farming, industry, and home use in developed and **developing countries**. In **developed countries**, there are many factories, so a lot of water is used in industry. In developing countries, more water is used for farming.

 People cannot grow crops without giving them water to help growth.

Different types of bar charts

These two bar charts show the same information, but in different ways. On the double bar chart (top), there is a different coloured bar for each type of country. The key shows what each colour represents. The **x-axis** shows the types of water use. You can see that industrial use is much higher in developed countries. In the stacked bar chart (bottom), each stack adds up to 100%. Like the double bar chart, the **y axis** shows percentages, but here the x-axis shows developed and developing countries. It is easy to see that farming is by far the biggest use of water in developing countries.

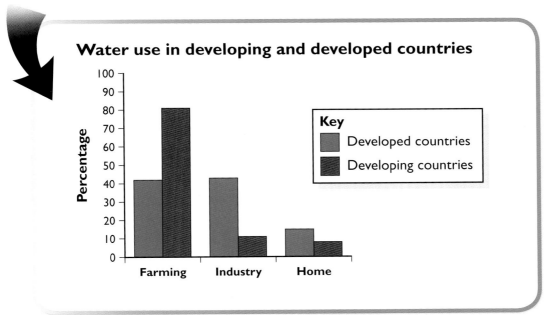

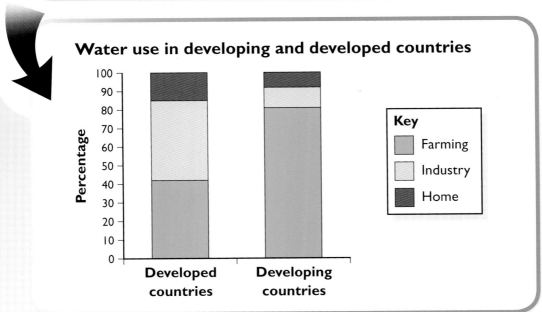

WATER AT HOME

In our homes, we are used to getting as much water as we need, at the turn of a tap. People use water at home for the most basic – and important – activities. Everyone needs to drink water, and water is used in cooking, too. People use water to wash their bodies and their clothes, and to flush the toilet. No one could clean a house or wash the dishes without water.

 We need water to clean our teeth, but turning off the tap when brushing helps us not to use too much.

 Having a shower instead of a bath is a great way to save water when we wash ourselves.

Water is also used outdoors, for example, to water plants in the garden, and to wash windows and cars. We also use water for less vital uses, such as filling swimming pools.

Humans need to consume more than two litres (four pints) of water each day just to make sure that our bodies work properly. This water is needed to digest food, clear our bodies of waste, and to keep our bodies healthy. People get some of this water by consuming drinks, such as plain water, fruit juice, milk, tea, and coffee. They also get water from food, especially fruit and vegetables.

Water, please!

The table below shows the percentage of water used for different activities in the home. All the percentages add up to 100 percent. The pie chart turns this information into a visual form. The different coloured sections show the percentage of the total amount of water that is used for each activity. The key shows the activity that each section represents. The pie chart shows at a glance that most water in the home is used for washing ourselves, followed closely by flushing the toilet.

Activity	Percentage of total water use in the home
Washing ourselves	33
Flushing the toilet	30
Washing clothes	13
Washing dishes	8
Drinking water	4
Outdoor use	7
Other	5
Total	100

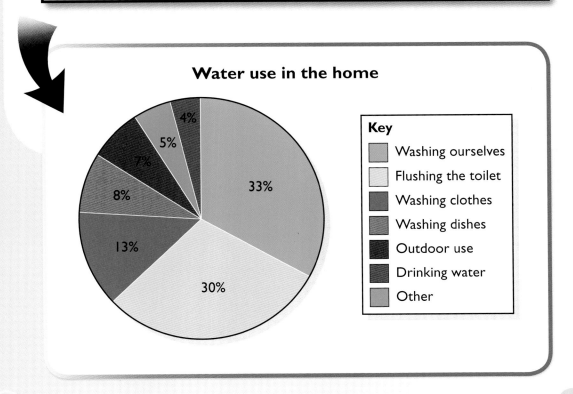

Water use in the home

Key
- Washing ourselves
- Flushing the toilet
- Washing clothes
- Washing dishes
- Outdoor use
- Drinking water
- Other

CLEAN WATER

Clean water is vital for farming, **industry**, and homes. Most of the Earth's water (97 percent) is salt water, which humans cannot use. Only three percent is fresh water. However, three-quarters of this is trapped in **glaciers** and **icecaps**. So less than one percent of the Earth's water is available for more than six billion people to use!

Water access

When we want clean water, we just turn on a tap. Water gets to our homes, schools, and work through pipes. However, only about half the world's population has access to clean water at home. Other people access fresh water from protected **springs** and **wells**.

More than one billion people in the world are forced to get their water from dirty wells or springs, or from lakes or rivers. Dirty water can cause illness and even death.

 In some parts of the world, the only available water is dirty water from muddy river beds.

Showing the smallest slices

We can link more than one pie chart to show more than one set of information about a subject. In this example, we can see how much of the Earth's water is usable, and where this water comes from. The pie chart at the top shows the percentage of water that is usable and not usable by humans. The second pie chart shows the breakdown of the smallest "slice" – the percentage of water that is usable. It shows where this usable water is found. The headings show the subjects of the two pie charts. Linking two pie charts allows us to see quickly that most of the Earth's water is not usable by humans, and that most of the water that humans can use comes from **groundwater**.

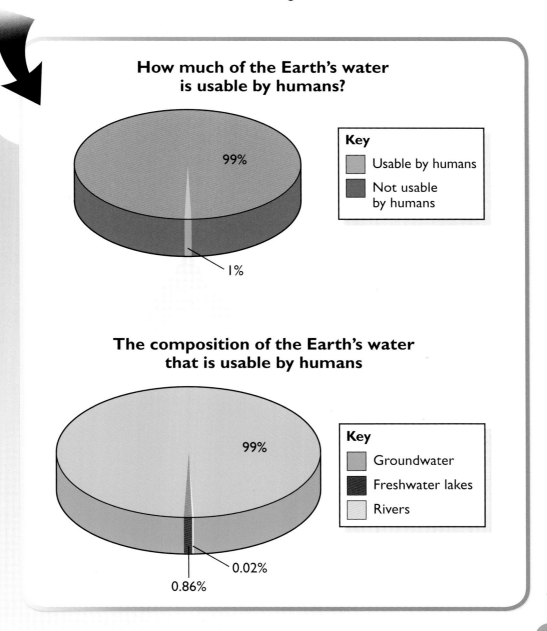

How much of the Earth's water is usable by humans?

99%

1%

Key

Usable by humans

Not usable by humans

The composition of the Earth's water that is usable by humans

99%

0.02%

0.86%

Key

Groundwater

Freshwater lakes

Rivers

People cannot live without water. Water is needed at home, and for **industry** and farming. Sometimes, water needs to be taken a long way to where it is needed. **Aqueducts** are one method of carrying water for long distances. The California Aqueduct in the United States is 444 miles (715 km) long!

Everyone needs to eat and, without water, farmers could not grow crops, such as rice, wheat, and vegetables, that people depend on. In countries where there is very little **precipitation**, growing crops can be almost impossible. Even in countries where levels of precipitation are good, farmers need to water crops so they can really thrive.

Irrigation

Irrigation is the best way for farmers to water crops. Irrigation has been used for thousands of years. In irrigation, pipes and ditches are used to take water to where crops are growing. Nowadays, these pipes are controlled by motors. Irrigation uses a lot of water.

 Irrigation is the easiest way to get much-needed water to growing crops.

Line graphs

A line graph is a type of graph that is used to show how something changes, for example, over a period of time. This line graph shows how irrigation increased in Bangladesh over the period from 1982 to 1998. Time is shown on the **x-axis**. The **y-axis** shows the amount of land that was irrigated, measured in millions of **hectares**. Dots are placed on the graph, showing the amount of land that was irrigated during each time period. They are then joined up to form a line. The line goes up from left to right, which shows that irrigation increased steadily.

Year	Irrigated land (millions of hectares)
1982–83	1.52
1985–86	1.74
1989–90	2.58
1993–94	2.94
1997–98	3.83

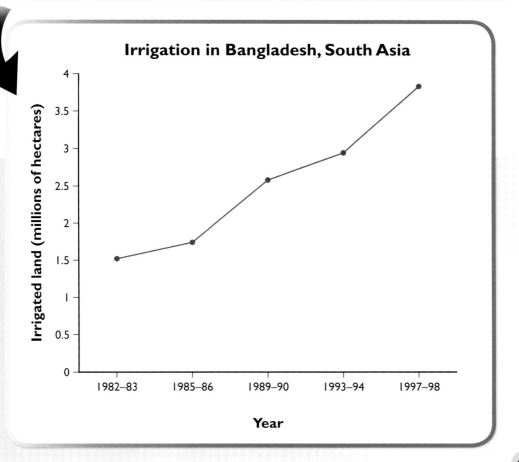

Most countries have at least a small amount of **precipitation**, though some get more than others. In some places, people collect rainwater that falls into rivers or lakes, and they are able to use this for all their needs. They do not have to pay for water.

However, in many countries, people have to pay to use water. They also pay to have water cleaned, so it is safe to use. Companies, called water suppliers, provide and clean water for **industry**, farming, and home use. In some places, clean water is cheap. In others, it is more expensive.

How do we get water?

Water suppliers normally get water from lakes, rivers, or **aquifers**. They then clean the water and store it in reservoirs. Sometimes, water suppliers add chemicals to water, to make it safer and healthier. They then send the water through pipes to where it is needed.

Once water has been used in people's homes, it goes into **sewers**, and the water suppliers clean it again in water treatment centres. Some of the cleaned water is sent back into lakes, rivers, or oceans through pipes. The rest of the cleaned water is sent to be used in industry or farming, where it is not as important for the water to be clean enough to drink.

 Reservoirs are like big lakes, which are used by water suppliers to store water until it is needed.

The price of water

The table below shows the cost of buying 1,000 litres (220 gallons) of water in 11 different countries. The prices are shown in US dollars. The bar chart puts the information in a visual form. In this bar chart, the bars are horizontal, rather than vertical. The **x-axis** shows the cost of 1,000 litres (220 gallons) of water in US dollars (US $). The **y-axis** shows the countries.

Country	Cost of 1,000 litres of water (US $)
Germany	2.25
UK	1.90
Belgium	1.72
France	1.58
Italy	1.15
Australia	1.01
South Africa	0.92
Canada	0.79
US	0.66
Libya	0.35
Taiwan	0.25

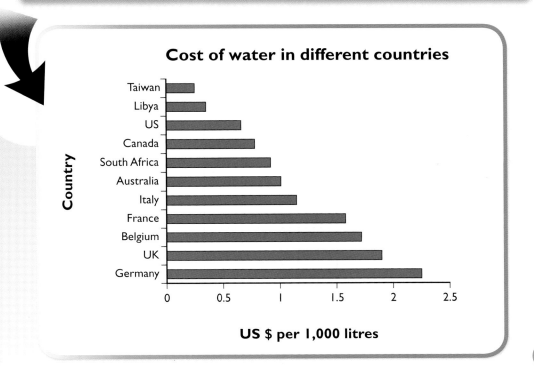

Cost of water in different countries

US $ per 1,000 litres

TOO LITTLE WATER

People can only use a tiny amount of the Earth's water. It can be hard to provide enough water to meet everyone's needs. Already, one in every five people does not have access to safe, clean water. By 2027, because there will be more people, we may need 40 percent more water than we do now.

People in **developed countries** use much more water than people in **developing countries**. In parts of the USA, for example, one person uses 1,000 litres (220 gallons) of water every day. That is 100 times more than one person in Mozambique, Africa.

 Water shortages will become more of a problem as the world's population increases.

Making a difference

This double bar chart shows how much water we can save by changing some of our daily habits. The blue bar shows how much water one person normally uses for different activities, for example, every time they brush their teeth. The green bar shows how much water they use when following the water-saving tips below. The **x-axis** shows the activities and the **y-axis** shows how much water is used.

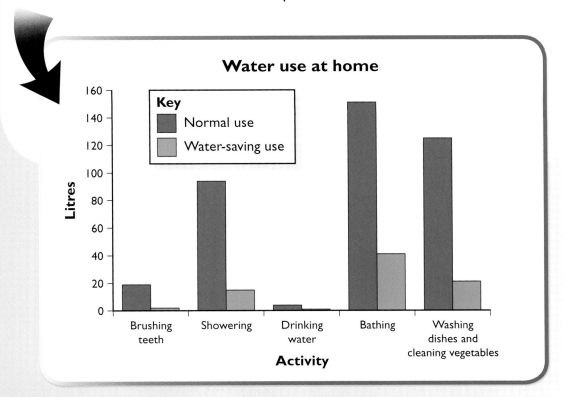

Water-saving tips

Saving water is important. By following these tips, one person could save 300 litres (500 pints) of water! In the bar chart you can see how much water can be saved by using these tips.

● Don't leave the tap running when brushing your teeth.

● Have showers instead of baths. In the shower, turn the water off whilst you put shampoo or soap on.

● If you have a bath, don't completely fill the bath tub with water.

● Keep a jug of drinking water in the fridge, so you don't need to wait for tap water to run cold.

● Don't wash dishes or clean vegetables under running water.

WATER POLLUTION

Water shortages and water **pollution** are causing a water crisis in the world. Water becomes polluted when one or more substances get into it, making it dirty. Water pollution can harm and kill plants and animals. It can cause illnesses that kill humans, too. Polluted water cannot be used safely by humans.

Causes of pollution

There are many causes of water pollution. In farming and **industry**, clean water is often taken from rivers and lakes, and then polluted with chemicals. When it is put back into the same rivers and lakes, it pollutes the rest of the water.

Sewage can also pollute water. In many countries, sewage is cleaned in water treatment centres. However, sewage that has not been cleaned is sometimes put into oceans, lakes, and rivers. Water that is polluted by sewage can cause serious illnesses, which kill millions of people every year.

Homes and transport are other causes of water pollution. When people throw away waste, it is often buried underground in landfills. **Groundwater** sources can be polluted when substances from the rotting waste leak into the ground. Oil and other chemicals leaked from cars, lorries, and ships can pollute water in rivers, lakes, and oceans.

 An oil spill from a damaged ship can pollute huge amounts of water.

 Water suppliers clean up water in water treatment centres, making it safe for human use.

A human problem

This pie chart shows how much water pollution is caused by different activities. It looks at the water pollution in 1999 in Northern Ireland as a whole. The sections of the pie chart break the pollution down into different activities: farming, industry, sewage, homes, transport, and other activities. The key shows what each coloured section represents. The pie chart shows that most of the water pollution was caused by industry, followed closely by farming.

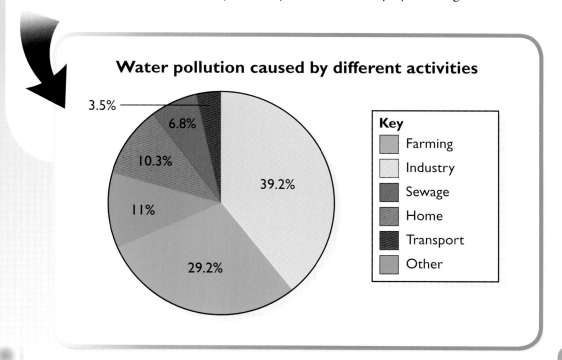

Water pollution caused by different activities

3.5%
6.8%
10.3%
11%
39.2%
29.2%

Key
- Farming
- Industry
- Sewage
- Home
- Transport
- Other

WATER FOR HEALTH

Every person in the world should have access to clean, safe water. People should also have access to good **sanitation**. People who do not have clean water may find it hard to grow the food they need. They may become ill – and even die – because of dirty water and poor sanitation.

Some organizations, such as UNICEF and WaterAid, help to teach people about safe water and sanitation. This can help people to protect themselves from disease.

Even simple things, such as washing hands before eating, can protect people.

Organizations also work with local people to provide the clean water and sanitation that is needed. Sometimes, people collect rainwater as it falls onto clean roofs. They may build **wells** to access **groundwater**. They may protect **springs** or build water tanks, so water can stay clean. People can also build toilets that are clean and safe to use.

 Building simple, clean toilets can prevent serious illness and save lives.

Stopping diarrhoea

Diarrhoea, caused by dirty water and poor sanitation, kills 1.8 million children under the age of five every year. However, many of these cases could be prevented. Clean water, and good sanitation and hygiene, can reduce the number of deaths by 65 percent. Simply washing hands with soap and clean water can reduce diarrhoea by more than 40 percent.

 Everyone in the world should have access to safe fresh water.

A vital resource

Water is very precious. Every single living thing needs fresh water for health – and life. Yet only 3 percent of the world's water is fresh water. It is important to work together to make sure that everyone has access to clean, safe water and sanitation. By using water carefully and preventing **pollution**, we can all help to protect the Earth's most vital resource.

Data is information about something. We often get important data as a mass of numbers, and it is difficult to make any sense of them. Graphs and charts are ways of displaying information visually. This helps us to see relationships and patterns in the data. Different types of graphs or charts are good for displaying different types of information.

Pie charts

A pie chart is used to show the different parts of a whole picture. A pie chart is the best way to show how something is divided up. These charts show information as different sized portions of a circle. They can help you compare proportions. You can easily see which section is the largest "slice" of the pie.

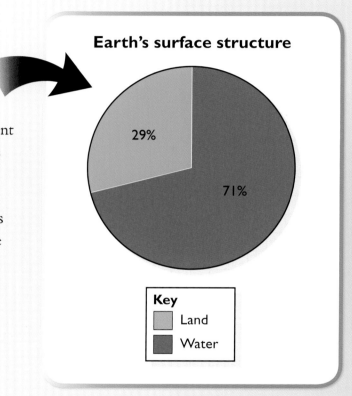

Earth's surface structure

29%

71%

Key
- Land
- Water

Bar charts

Bar charts are a good way to compare amounts of different things. Bar charts have a vertical **y-axis** showing the scale, and a horizontal **x-axis** showing the different types of information. They can show one or more different types of bars.

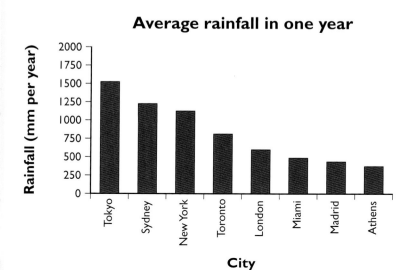

Average rainfall in one year

Rainfall (mm per year)

2000
1750
1500
1250
1000
750
500
250
0

Tokyo · Sydney · New York · Toronto · London · Miami · Madrid · Athens

City

Stacked bar charts

A stacked bar chart provides more information than a simple bar chart. Each bar in a stacked bar chart is like a rectangular pie chart. It makes it easy to compare different sets of percentages.

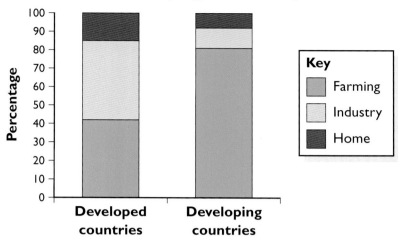

Water use in developing and developed countries

Line graphs

Line graphs use lines to join up points on a graph. They can be used to show how something changes over time. If you put several lines on one line graph, you can compare the overall pattern of several sets of data. Time, such as months, is usually shown on the x-axis.

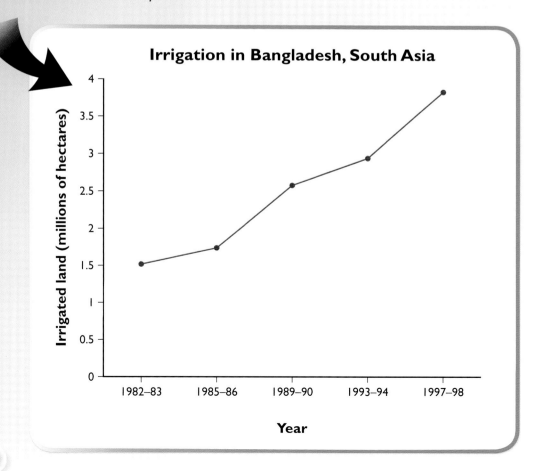

Irrigation in Bangladesh, South Asia

GLOSSARY

aqueduct structure used to carry water through pipes. It sometimes looks like a high bridge with a lot of arches

aquifer body of rock that holds water, or through which water flows

atom one of the tiny building blocks that make up all matter

condense change from a gas to a liquid

data information, often in the form of numbers

developed country country where many people are relatively well-off and work in offices or in new technology, rather than producing food or raw materials

developing country country where most people have little money and work either on farms or in industries producing raw materials

drought long period of time with very little or no precipitation

evaporate change from a liquid to a gas

flood large amount of water covering land that is usually dry

gas form of matter that has no definite shape or size. Air is made up of gases.

glacier large mass of ice that moves slowly

groundwater water that is held under the ground in soil and rocks

hectare area equal to 10,000 square metres

hydrogen type of gas, which is very light. It combines with oxygen to form water

icecap thick layer of ice that covers land all the time

industry businesses and activities that produce goods for sale

irrigation supplying water to land, so that plants and crops can grow

liquid form of matter that has no definite shape and can be poured easily

molecule group of two or more atoms joined together

oxygen type of gas which is needed for all life on Earth to survive. It combines with hydrogen to form water.

polar regions areas around the North Pole and the South Pole, where it is very cold all year round

pollution dirty material added to water by waste or dangerous substances

precipitation moisture that falls from the sky. It may be rain, sleet, hail, or snow.

run-off when water flows downhill into rivers, lakes, and oceans

sanitation system for taking dirty water and sewage away from buildings

sewage waste water from sinks and toilets

sewer large pipe for carrying waste water and sewage

solid form of matter that has a definite shape

spring place where water naturally flows out from the ground

swamp area of shallow water standing over wet land

transpiration process in which plants lose water through their leaves

water cycle circulation of water, in its different forms, from the Earth's surface to the air, and then back to Earth again

water vapour gas form of water, which forms when water is heated up

well hole in the ground from which people can collect water

x-axis horizontal line on a graph

y-axis vertical line on a graph

Further Information

Books

Help the Environment: Saving Water, Charlotte Guillain (Heinemann Library, 2008)

Our World: Oceans, Valerie Bodden (Creative Education, 2006)

Planet Earth: Weather and Climate, Jim Pipe (Ticktock Media Ltd, 2008)

Websites

United Nations Environment Programme has plenty of information on caring for the environment.
www.unep.org/tunza/children

This is the United States Environmental Protection Agency's section for children about water.
www.epa.gov/waterscience/KidsStuff/

WaterAid has games and information about water on its website.
www.wateraid.org/uk/learn_zone/pupils_under_11/default.asp